■SCHOLASTIC
News
Nonfiction Readers

Dinosaur Dig!

by Susan H. Gray

Children's Press®
A Division of Scholastic Inc.
New York Toronto London Auckland Sydney
Mexico City New Delhi Hong Kong
Danbury, Connecticut

These content vocabulary word builders are for grades 1–2.

Subject Consultant: Rudyard W. Sadleir, Doctoral Candidate in Evolutionary Biology, University of Chicago, Chicago, Illinois

Reading Consultant: Cecilia Minden-Cupp, PhD, Former Director of the Language and Literacy Program, Harvard Graduate School of Education, Cambridge, Massachusetts

Book Design: Simonsays Design!
Book Production: The Design Lab

Library of Congress Cataloging-in-Publication Data
Gray, Susan Heinrichs.
Dinosaur dig! / by Susan H. Gray.
    p. cm. — (Scholastic news nonfiction readers)
Includes bibliographical references and index.
ISBN-13: 978-0-531-17482-1
ISBN-10: 0-531-17482-4
1. Paleontology—Juvenile literature. 2. Dinosaurs—Juvenile literature. I. Title. II. Series.
QE714.5.G73 2007
567.9—dc22   2006024049

CONTENTS

WORD HUNT

Look for these words as you read. They will be in **bold**.

chisels
(**chiz**-uhlz)

paleontologists
(pale-ee-uhn-
tol-uh-jists)

plaster
(**plass**-tur)

dinosaur
(**dye**-nuh-sawr)

fossils
(**foss**-uhlz)

rock hammers
(rok **ham**-urz)

skeleton
(**skell**-uh-tuhn)

WHERE ARE WE GOING?

We packed our clothes. We packed our maps and cameras. We have hammers and paintbrushes. We even have dentist tools. Where are we going? We're going on a **dinosaur** dig!

dinosaur

People search for dinosaur bones along the Red Deer River in Alberta, Canada.

We drive to a dig site. It is a place where **paleontologists** have found many dinosaur bone **fossils**. Fossils are the remains of living things from millions of years ago. Paleontologists are the people who study fossils.

fossils

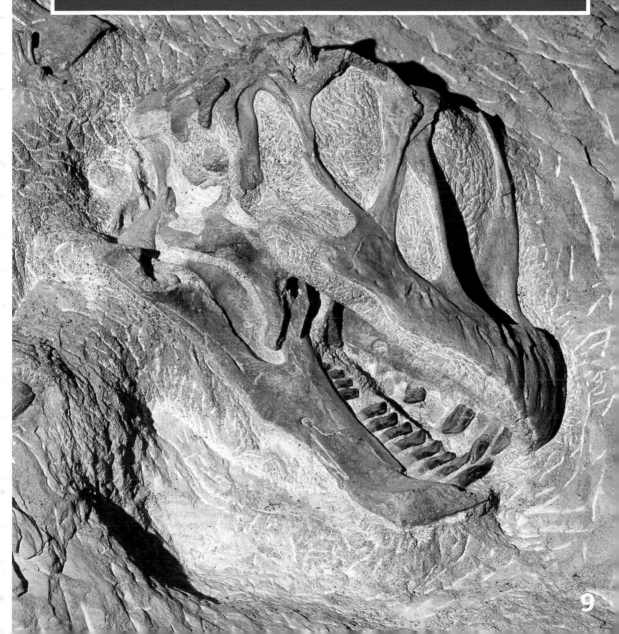

This dinosaur skull was found at Dinosaur National Monument in Utah.

We see some huge bones buried in rock! What kind of bones do you think they are?

First, we take pictures of our discovery. Then we get our **rock hammers** and start chipping at the rock. Soon the bones break free!

rock hammer

A paleontologist uses a rock hammer to dig out a fossil.

The bones are a mess. Chunks of rock are stuck to them. We use hammers and **chisels** to knock off the big chunks.

Dentist tools remove the little chunks. Paintbrushes clean off the dirt.

chisels

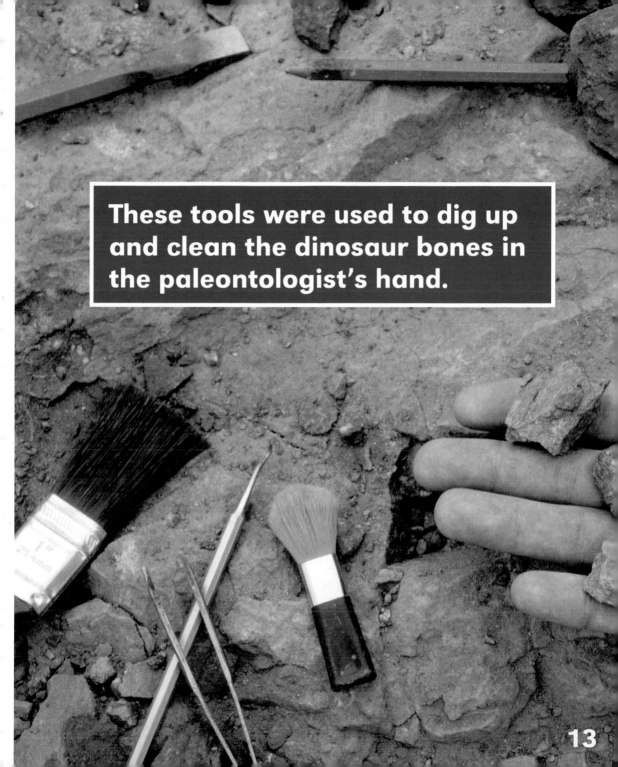

These tools were used to dig up and clean the dinosaur bones in the paleontologist's hand.

Some fossil bones break easily. We must protect them.

First, we wrap the bones in foil or wet paper towels. Next, we mix a paste that hardens when it dries called **plaster**.

Then we cover the bones with strips of cloth soaked in plaster. The plaster dries with the bones safely inside.

Workers wrap cloth strips soaked in plaster around a large dinosaur bone.

On our dig, we find hundreds of bones. We put the little ones in boxes. We coat the big ones with plaster.

We carefully pack everything and return home. Then we will have more work to do.

Drawing maps of where the bones are found helps us identify the bones and put them back together.

We cut away the plaster and clean the bones. Do you think we can put all of these bones together?

It's not easy, but we begin building a **skeleton**. We use wires and rods to hold everything in place.

The job takes months. But, at last, we have a dinosaur!

Workers build a *Barosaurus* skeleton.

19

WHAT SHOULD WE TAKE ON OUR DIG?

Take a look at the items on this page. Choose the six that you would take with you on a dinosaur dig.

sunscreen

notebook and pencil

sunglasses

bottled water

handheld video games

assorted paleontology tools

skateboard

camera and film

YOUR NEW WORDS

chisels (**chiz**-uhlz) tools with a sharp edge used to chip away rock

dinosaur (**dye**-nuh-sawr) a scaly skinned animal that lived millions of years ago

fossils (**foss**-uhlz) remains of plants or animals from millions of years ago

paleontologists (pale-ee-uhn-**tol**-uh-jists) scientists who study fossils to learn about animals and plants that lived millions of years ago

plaster (**plass**-tur) a mixture of water and a fine powdery material that hardens when it dries

rock hammers (rok **ham**-urz) special hammers that have a pick on one side of the head

skeleton (**skell**-uh-tuhn) the entire set of bones of an animal

SOME DINOSAUR BONES

backbone

foot

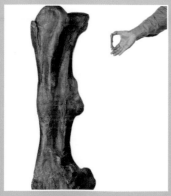

leg

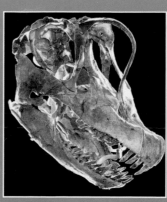

skull

INDEX

FIND OUT MORE

Book:
Ripley, Esther. *The Big Dinosaur Dig.* New York: DK Publishing, 2003.

Website:
Dinosaur Dig: Finding Fossils
http://www.sdnhm.org/kids/fossils/index.html

MEET THE AUTHOR

Susan H. Gray has a master's degree in zoology. She has written more than seventy science and reference books for children. She especially loves to write about animals. Susan and her husband, Michael, live in Cabot, Arkansas.